W9-BXH-030

Just the Facts
STDs

Sean Connolly

Heinemann Library
Chicago, Illinois

Customer Service 888-454-2279
Visit our website at www.heinemannlibrary.com

Designed by M2 Graphic Design
Originated by Ambassador Litho
Printed in China by South China Printers

07 06 05
10 9 8 7 6 5 4 3 2

Library of Congress Cataloging-in-Publication Data
Connolly, Sean.
  STDs / Sean Connolly.
      p. cm. -- (Just the facts)
Includes bibliographical references and index.
  ISBN 1-58810-681-0
  1. Sexually transmitted diseases--Juvenile literature. [1. Sexually transmitted diseases. 2. Diseases.] I. Title. II. Series.
  RC200.25 .C66 2002
  616.95'1--dc21
                                         2001006072

Acknowledgments
The author and publishers are grateful to the following for permission to reproduce copyright material: pp. 6, 35 Rex Features; pp. 7, 14, 21, 22, 23, 24, 25, 27, 29, 30, 32, 44, 47 Robert Harding Picture Library; p. 9 Science Photo Library; p. 11 Panos Pictures; pp. 13, 15, 17, 33, 38 Corbis; p. 18 Eyewire; pp. 37, 48, 49 Corbis Stock Market; p. 40, 42 Popperfoto; p. 41 Getty (Telegraph Colour Library); p. 50 Stone; p. 51 Colin Hockley.
Cover photographs by Tudor Photography, Image 100, and Telegraph Colour Library.

Every effort has been made to contact copyright holders of any material reproduced in this book. Any omissions will be rectified in subsequent printings if notice is given to the publisher.

Some words are shown in bold, **like this.** You can find out what they mean by looking in the glossary.

Contents

STDs 4

What Are STDs? 6

Epidemic Proportions? 10

History of STDs 12

A Special Case 16

Who Contracts STDs? 18

How STDs Work 22

Checklist of Common STDs 24

Life with STDs 32

Family and Friends 36

Control and Prevention 40

Lessons from HIV and AIDS 42

Treatment and Counseling 46

People to Talk To 50

Information and Advice 52

More Books to Read 53

Glossary 54

Index 56

STDs

The dawn of the 21st century has brought with it an exciting array of scientific advances. People eat better, remain healthier, and live longer than at any other time in history. So it seems strange that we are still trying to combat some of the same curable diseases that affected people more than 2,000 years ago. Yet that is where we stand with gonorrhea, one of the 25 or so sexually transmitted diseases (STDs). Although it is sexual contact that spreads these diseases from one person to another, it is ignorance about them that really allows them to flourish. Too few people—even some who are themselves infected—follow the simple medical advice on how to prevent STD infection.

Knowing the enemy

This book aims to overturn some of that ignorance. It looks at the recent rise in STDs, especially since the well-publicized spread of **HIV** and **AIDS**—a sexually transmitted disease. As recently as the late 1970s, many medical experts were predicting that curable STDs such as syphilis would be wiped out. That has not happened, and since then more than a dozen other new STDs have been identified.

The following pages offer an explanation of what STDs are, as well as how they can be prevented and treated. No matter what form they take—**virus, bacteria,** or insect—they all pass from person to person in the same way. What happens after that depends on the disease itself, and many STDs mask their arrival for a long time.

The core of this book deals closely with six of the most common STDs. They also represent three of the main types of sexually transmitted disease: viral, bacterial, and insect. It examines them closely, providing details on their **symptoms, diagnosis,** and treatment. Just as importantly, this book offers advice on how to deal personally with STD infections, how to talk to others about the issue, and where to find **confidential** advice and counseling.

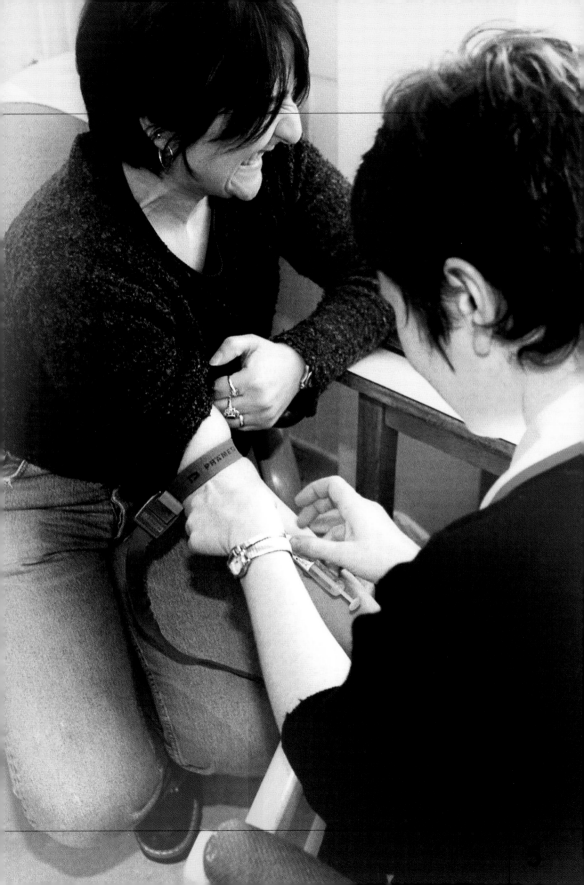

What Are STDs?

Sexually transmitted diseases (STDs) are **infections** that can be spread by having sex with another person who is infected. They are among the most common **infectious** diseases in the world today. More than 24 STDs have now been identified. Most of these are curable, although some are not. Many people who have an STD do not even know it. They may look healthy, but they still could have an STD. Some people do not tell their sexual partner, even if they know they have an STD.

Secrecy and shame

Until the late 20th century, STDs were known as **venereal diseases** or simply VD. Although these diseases were quite widespread, many people preferred not to discuss them. Soldiers and sailors sometimes received a brief pep talk about the dangers of **contracting** syphilis or gonorrhea—two of the most common STDs—but the subject rarely was taught in schools. As a result, few people knew much about the diseases or how to prevent or treat them.

Unfortunately, this ignorance and air of secrecy continued well into the 1960s and even beyond. That era brought many changes in people's sexual behavior. One of the most important changes since that time is that young people are becoming sexually active earlier in life, yet marrying later. This combination means that, overall, people now have more sexual partners in their lives. With the increase in sexual partners comes the increased risk of contracting—or infecting someone else with—a sexually transmitted disease.

The Woodstock Festival in 1969 was typical of the decade when a new era of sexual freedom was beginning.

The hidden foe

Many **organisms** cause these diseases. Most of them are too small to be seen with the naked eye, except for pubic lice—tiny insects that live and breed in the pubic hair around a person's genital area. **Bacteria** and **viruses** are two common types of organisms that cause infection as they pass from one person to another in body fluids. **Fungi** and even yeasts can also cause STDs. Most of the time, STDs cause no **symptoms,** particularly in women. Some people can confuse STD symptoms with those of other diseases not transmitted through sexual contact. Even when an STD causes no symptoms, an infected person may be able to pass the disease on to a sexual partner. That is why many doctors recommend regular testing for people who have more than one sexual partner.

A micrograph (photo of a microscopic image) shows the presence of *Chlamydia trachomatis* bacteria, which causes a common STD.

The risks for women

Although STDs are dangerous for whoever develops them, women face particular risks. The early **symptoms** of some STDs are hardly noticeable in women, since their sexual organs are inside their bodies. Men, on the other hand, can often detect early symptoms because their sexual organ (the penis) is easily visible. Other risks are directly related to the female **reproductive system.** Some STDs can spread into the uterus (womb) and Fallopian tubes to cause pelvic inflammatory disease (PID). This serious condition can cause both **infertility** and complications if the woman becomes pregnant. Some of these complications can be fatal.

Approximately 15 percent of all infertile women are infertile because of damage caused by PID. Other STDs may also lead to cervical cancer in women. They can also pass from a mother to her baby before, during, or immediately after birth. Although some of these infections of the newborn can be cured easily, others may cause a baby to be permanently disabled or even to die.

Using our knowledge

Understanding the basic facts about STDs—the ways in which they are spread, their common symptoms, and how they can be treated—is the first step toward prevention. If they are detected and treated early, many STDs can be treated effectively. Some can even be cured. However, other infections have become resistant to the drugs used to treat them and now require newer types of medicine. Recent research suggests that having some types of STD actually increases the risk of being infected with the **HIV** virus, which in turn leads to **AIDS.**

❝STDs [are] hidden epidemics of tremendous health and economic consequence in the United States. They represent a growing threat to the nation's health, and national action is urgently needed.❞

(1997 Institute of Medicine report)

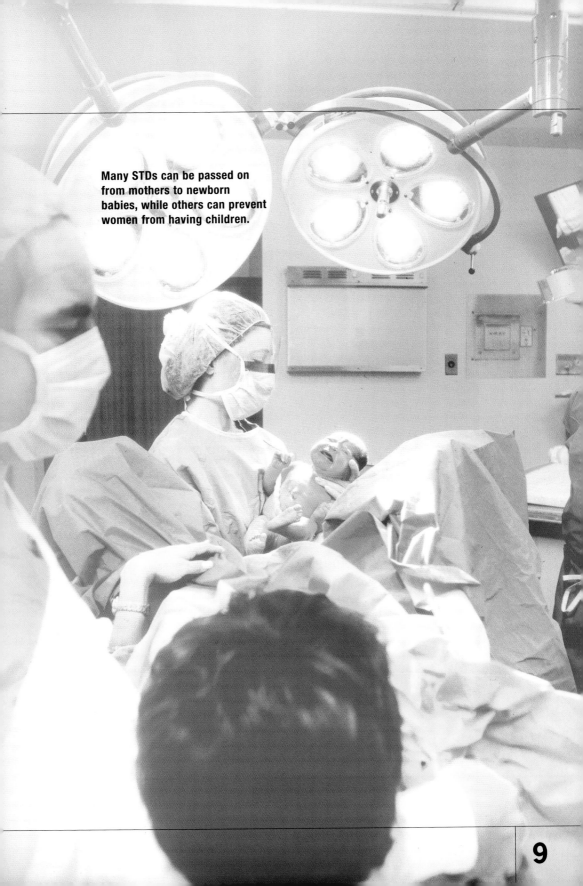

Many STDs can be passed on from mothers to newborn babies, while others can prevent women from having children.

Epidemic Proportions?

An **epidemic** is a disease that affects many people at the same time, spreading from person to person in a place that does not normally have that disease. Many **infectious** diseases, such as flu, spread as epidemics. It seems clear that many sexually transmitted diseases are expanding along these lines. At least 25 STDs have been identified so far; these are all on the increase and new variations are regularly found. The question is: How widespread are they?

Keeping tabs

Four of the most widespread STDs are curable. They are: gonorrhea, chlamydial infection, syphilis, and trichomoniasis. As the public has become more aware of the possible cures, more infected people are reporting to clinics for treatment. It is only in these closely observed conditions—with patients registered and treatments **monitored**—that health officials can keep an accurate number of affected people.

The figures that they have amassed confirm that there does seem to be an epidemic. Recent figures compiled by the World Health Organization have shown more than 330 million new cases of these four diseases each year for the past decade.

According to 2002 statistics from the Centers for Disease Control and Prevention, more than 65 million people in the United States are currently living with an incurable sexually transmitted disease. An additional 15 million people become infected with one or more STDs each year, roughly half of whom contract lifelong infections. Approximately 25 percent of all new STD infections are in teenagers.

Armed with the results of field experience (awareness of how the diseases progress), health officials can also predict some STD side effects. For example, between 10 and 40 percent of women infected with gonorrhea will go on to develop pelvic inflammatory disease (see page 8) unless they receive early treatment.

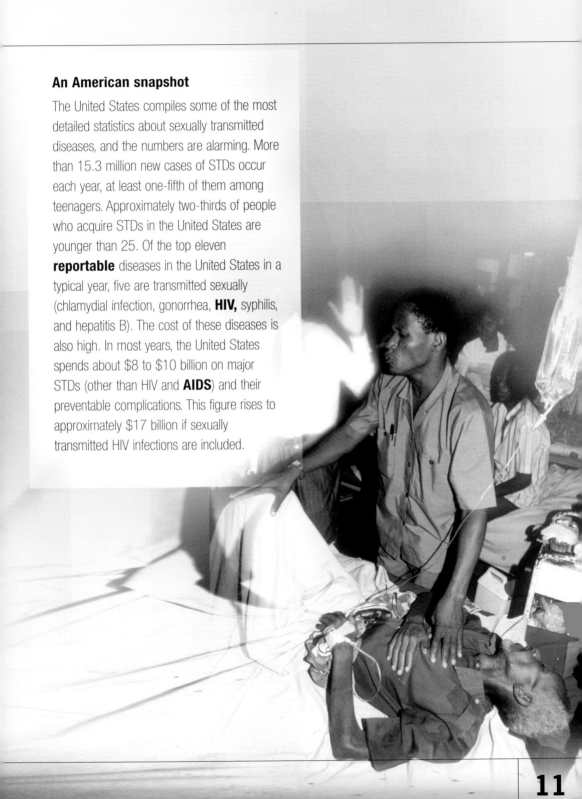

An American snapshot

The United States compiles some of the most detailed statistics about sexually transmitted diseases, and the numbers are alarming. More than 15.3 million new cases of STDs occur each year, at least one-fifth of them among teenagers. Approximately two-thirds of people who acquire STDs in the United States are younger than 25. Of the top eleven **reportable** diseases in the United States in a typical year, five are transmitted sexually (chlamydial infection, gonorrhea, **HIV,** syphilis, and hepatitis B). The cost of these diseases is also high. In most years, the United States spends about $8 to $10 billion on major STDs (other than HIV and **AIDS**) and their preventable complications. This figure rises to approximately $17 billion if sexually transmitted HIV infections are included.

History of STDs

People have passed diseases on to each other sexually for as long as we can tell. Many distinct STDs might once have been considered as simply different forms of the same disease. Nevertheless, they were definitely understood to be linked to sexual conduct.

Gonorrhea is mentioned in some of the earliest writings in many cultures. The ancient Chinese recognized it and tried many remedies, including **acupuncture,** to treat it. The same disease is mentioned in the Old Testament of the Christian Bible. Ancient Jewish doctors advised people to wash with special soaps if they touched someone **infected** with the disease.

New arrival?

People in **medieval** Europe viewed gonorrhea as something to be feared and avoided, but not something that they understood. Many people believed that the disease, like other dangerous illnesses such as the **plague,** was a punishment from God.

Although there is now some evidence (see page 15) suggesting otherwise, many experts believe that syphilis was first introduced into Europe in 1493 by crew members returning from Christopher Columbus's first expedition to America. Within a few decades, it had become a major public disease. It was around this time that Paracelsus, a famous German doctor and chemist, began to argue that the new disease was somehow spread from person to person. Although he could find no cure for the disease—or even identify the real cause of it—his views gained importance over the next few centuries. People began to understand how syphilis (and gonorrhea) spread through sexual contact. Condoms and other protective devices became more common.

Columbus's crew encountered Native Americans, who many Europeans blamed for the spread of syphilis to Europe.

Effective treatment

By the early 20th century, medical science had a better idea of how diseases were passed on generally. Powerful microscopes and new medicines enabled researchers to identify **viruses** and **bacteria**—the causes of many diseases. In 1905, the German scientist Fritz Schaudinn discovered the **bacterium** that is responsible for syphilis. A year later, another German scientist, August von Wassermann, developed the first blood test to check for the disease in a patient. In 1909, a third German scientist, Paul Ehrlich, discovered the first effective treatment for syphilis: the arsenic-containing **compound** Salvarsan. Salvarsan did work well against syphilis, but it was expensive to produce and never became widespread as a treatment. The real breakthrough came when the **antibiotic** penicillin was first observed. Although this medicine was first discovered in 1928, it took another decade for the medical world to produce enough of it to be distributed widely.

Tests in the early 1940s showed that penicillin was highly effective against syphilis, gonorrhea, and other bacteria-related STDs. It remains the preferred treatment for syphilis. New varieties need to be developed to deal with strains of gonorrhea that have become **resistant** to the drug.

Paul Ehrlich, shown here with Japanese scientist Sahachiro Hata, made the medical breakthrough in the treatment of syphilis.

Health posters during World War II warned soldiers of the risks of contracting STDs, or *venereal diseases* (VD), as they were then known.

TO TRAINS

TAKING VD HOME TOO, SAILOR?

Dealing with the problem

Penicillin and other **antibiotics,** of course, only work against **bacteria** and have no effect on viral STDs such as hepatitis B and herpes. However, after World War II, the penicillin treatment began to achieve real success against the two main STDs of the time, syphilis and gonorrhea. The number of syphilis cases reported in the United States fell from 106,000 in 1947 to 25,000 in 1975.

Working against this successful trend was the change in sexual thinking that took hold in the 1960s and 1970s. STDs became more widespread as sexual attitudes became freer, and also because many people believed (wrongly) that the diseases had been wiped out. The arrival of **HIV** and **AIDS** in the 1980s distracted much attention away from traditional STDs, and health officials are still dealing with dangerous increases in nearly every sexually transmitted disease today.

Early precautions

The ancient Egyptians were familiar with condoms and used a linen sheath to protect against diseases. Silk was the preferred material for Chinese condoms, while the Japanese used leather and tortoiseshell sheaths. Men in ancient Rome used condoms made from goat bladders. Europeans in the 18th century used a variety of materials for their condoms, preferring those made from silk, linen, and lamb gut.

Challenging history

Female bones dug up in a churchyard in Rivenhall, England, are thought to disprove the long-standing belief that Christopher Columbus was responsible for importing syphilis into Europe in the late 15th century. **Archaeologists** have unearthed the skeleton of a woman, aged between 25 and 50, who suffered from this **sexually transmitted disease** at least 50 years before Columbus discovered America in 1492. Scientists are 95 percent certain that the woman, who is believed to have **contracted** the disease up to a decade before her death, lived in the **medieval** settlement some time between 1290 and 1445.

A Special Case

By the late 1970s, the world had become more familiar with the range and dangers of sexually transmitted diseases. New STDs, such as the herpes **virus,** gained a lot of publicity, and campaigns were started to make the public more aware of both precautions and prevention. Then, in the early 1980s, a new disease, which we now know as **AIDS,** began to sweep across the world. The causes of AIDS remained a mystery for several years, although it became apparent that the condition seemed to be a deadly STD. AIDS seemed at first to be confined to the gay community in major cities, but it soon became clear that the condition was also linked to **heterosexual** relations.

Increased awareness

In the two decades since AIDS was first identified worldwide, many books have been written on the subject. There has also been a great deal of important research. Most scientists now link the deadly condition of AIDS—which leaves the body open to **infection** from many sources—with a particular virus. It is this virus, known as the Human Immunodeficiency Virus (**HIV**), that is passed on from one person to another. An HIV-positive person—that is, somebody infected with the HIV virus—can infect someone else. The virus moves to another human when bodily fluids from an infected person pass to another person.

One of the major ways in which fluids pass from person to person is through sexual contact. For that reason, AIDS (and the HIV infection that leads to it) qualifies as a sexually transmitted disease. There are other ways in which this infection can be passed—through sharing needles, infected blood, and even in a mother's milk—but it is the sexual transmission of the virus that worries medical experts most.

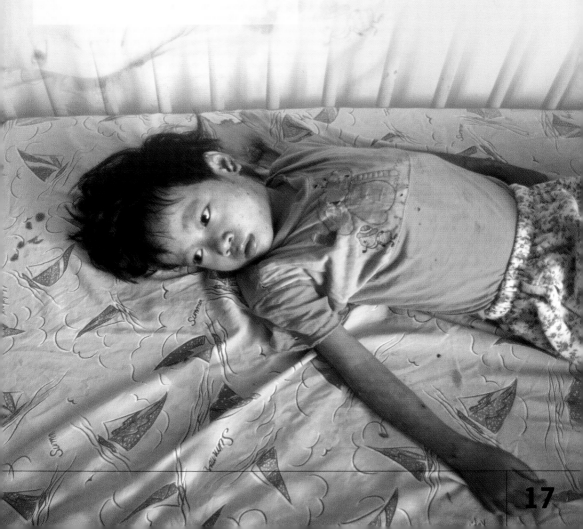

Hopes and fears

A number of treatments have been discovered to slow the spread of HIV in infected people, but there is no cure for the infection or the deadly AIDS condition that follows it. With the number of people now infected (roughly 40 million at the beginning of 2002) continuing to rise, the problem has become critical.

Who Contracts STDs?

Back in the days when sexually transmitted diseases were called **venereal diseases,** most people chose not to consider or even discuss the problem. Young people rarely heard of the diseases and their effects. At the same time, many parents chose to believe that the diseases were mainly the problem of other people—the poor, the badly brought up, uneducated people, or those living in inner cities. This almost deliberate ignorance of the diseases led to what has been described as a "culture of secrecy." The modern view of sexually transmitted diseases is to be more aware, open, and informative. This helps make knowledge far more available to the general public—young and old alike. With the knowledge we have gained, we can see that many of the old ideas about STDs were inaccurate, and allowed the diseases to spread.

It is important to remember that anyone, regardless of economic or social background, is at risk when it comes to STDs.

No boundaries

We know now that anyone who is having a sexual relationship can contract a sexually transmitted disease. It doesn't matter who you are so much as how you behave. STDs affect men and women of all backgrounds and economic levels. They are most common among teenagers and young adults. In fact, nearly two-thirds of all STDs occur in people younger than 25 years of age.

Although the treatments for the many STDs vary, much of the advice for preventing them remains the same. "Safe sex" advice, which has become more widely known throughout the **HIV** and **AIDS epidemic,** holds true with all other STDs. People should be prepared to use condoms (when they have sex) or choose to avoid sexual intercourse or other risky actions. They should be aware of the various diseases and their **symptoms** so that they can be tested (and treated if necessary) before it is too late. This advice is the same for anyone, anywhere.

Sometimes all of this encouragement to "be sensible" almost gets lost among the other messages competing for young people's attention. For nearly four decades, sex has become more widely discussed, and people can easily take it for granted or consider it "no big deal." It can be hard for young people, the group with the highest risk of contracting STDs, to remember the need to be cautious and sensible.

The road ahead

Despite our increased awareness of STDs—and with it, an increased willingness to talk about them—more needs to be done. The world as a whole is far from understanding the full picture about these diseases, and the diseases continue to increase. The Committee on Prevention and Control of Sexually Transmitted Diseases, part of the U.S. Institute of Medicine, has described STDs as "the Hidden **Epidemic.**" This term seems fitting, and also tragic, because many people might contract curable STDs, such as syphilis and gonorrhea, but not recognize the symptoms until it is too late to prevent lasting damage. Others, particularly women (see far right), run the risk of developing fatal conditions and even of passing them on to their babies.

❝Our society bombards our kids with all kinds of tantalizing images through television, music, film, and advertising. But there isn't much out there that balances these messages with sexuality awareness, responsibility, and sound judgement. Since sexuality is a fact of life at an early age, we must approach these hot topics with realistic communication, pointing out what it all means—including the potentially bad stuff like STDs.❞

(Dr. Linda Alexander, president of the American Social Health Association)

Dangers for women

Women have a higher chance of getting an STD than men. Young women, who are generally the most sexually active female age group, have more chance of getting an STD than older women. Worse still, women are more likely than men to have serious health problems that develop from STDs. Three of the most important are:

- pelvic inflammatory disease (PID)—an infection in the uterus, ovaries, and Fallopian tubes that can cause **infertility** (not being able to get pregnant) or an ectopic pregnancy (a pregnancy that occurs in the Fallopian tubes instead of the uterus)
- human papilloma virus (HPV)—an **infection** that can lead to cervical cancer
- infant death or disability—mothers with STDs can infect their babies. Some babies die from the infection and other babies are born with serious health problems.

This microscopic view shows a close-up of human papilloma viruses, which can lead to serious complications in women.

How STDs Work

As their name suggests, sexually transmitted diseases are passed on from one person to another through sexual relations. Tiny disease-causing substances travel in the fluids that are exchanged during sex. None of this is obvious at the time, though, and many people with an STD do not even know they have it. The **symptoms** are often barely even noticeable. Women, whose sexual organs are internal, find it very hard to notice the early symptoms. Even when they do notice something unusual, they might mistake the symptoms for one of the conditions affecting the **urinary tract.**

The pain and discomfort of these diseases is not confined to the genital area, where they usually enter the body. If left untreated, many STDs can lead to serious—and even deadly—problems elsewhere in the body.

The root of the problem

Just what causes sexually transmitted diseases and leads to such a variety of them? Nearly all of the known STDs are caused by tiny **organisms,** which live and breed inside, or on the surface of, the human body. Some are caused by **bacteria.** Medicines known as **antibiotics** can cure **infections** caused

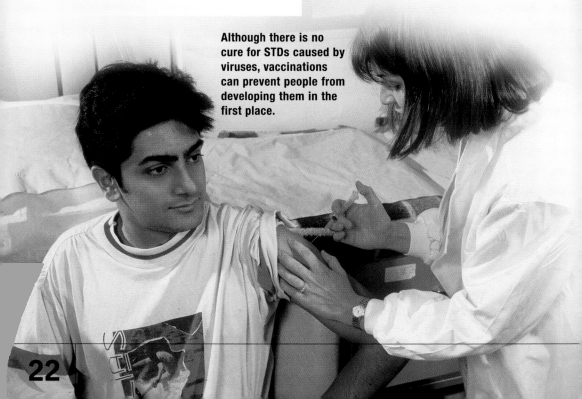

Although there is no cure for STDs caused by viruses, vaccinations can prevent people from developing them in the first place.

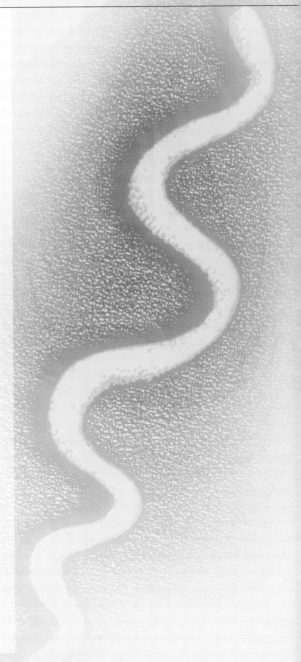

by bacteria, but there can be lasting damage done to a person's body if the infection is not caught soon enough. Others are caused by the spread of **viruses.** There is no cure for infections caused by viruses, but **vaccinations** can prevent people from becoming infected in the first place. Another group is caused by the spread of either tiny animals (such as insects) or **fungal** infection. Medicines can treat these infections and soothe the discomfort caused by them.

No matter what the source of the STD, though, it is the sexual act that provides a way of keeping the organism alive and allowing it to find a new home in another body. If any of the organisms causing STDs were removed from the body, they would soon die.

The following pages describe six of the most common STDs. Three of them (chlamydial infection, gonorrhea, and syphilis) are caused by bacteria. Genital herpes and hepatitis are caused by viruses. The last STD covered in the next section, pubic lice, is a condition caused by the spread of tiny insects.

This micrograph shows the distinctive spiral shape of *Treponema pallidum*, the bacterium that causes syphilis.

Checklist of Common STDs

Chlamydial infection

Chlamydial infection is caused by a **bacterium** called *Chlamydia trachomatis.* It is one of the most widespread bacterial STDs in the world. Because chlamydial infection does not make most people sick, you can have it and not know it. This makes the **infection** even more frightening.

Symptoms

The **symptoms,** which are usually very mild, normally appear within one to three weeks after being infected. An infected person may have an abnormal **discharge (mucus** or pus) from the vagina or penis, or pain while urinating. Some people also develop pain along the lining of the eye.

Diagnosis

Chlamydial infection is easily confused with gonorrhea because the symptoms of both diseases are similar. The best way to find out whether the infection is chlamydial is through laboratory tests. A doctor sends a sample of mucus from the vagina or penis to a laboratory that will look for the **bacteria.**

Treatment

Doctors can treat the infection with a choice of **antibiotics.** The infection may move inside the body if it is not treated. There, it can cause pelvic inflammatory disease (PID) in women and **epididymitis** in men, two very serious illnesses. Babies can develop pneumonia and eye problems if their mother is infected.

Urine tests, such as this one checking for the presence of hepatitis viruses, are a useful way of testing for a range of STDs.

Genital herpes

Genital herpes is caused by one of the herpes **viruses.** Another variation of the herpes virus causes cold sores. The genital variety causes blisters and sores that can take weeks to heal. Just like cold sores, these blisters can flare up again unexpectedly. Since it is a virus, it stays in the body indefinitely. However, the number of outbreaks tends to go down over a period of years.

Symptoms

The infection is usually hard to detect because there are few immediate symptoms. When they do occur, they appear as one or more blisters on or around the genitals or rectum. These break, leaving tender sores that may take two to four weeks to heal the first time they occur. Another outbreak can appear weeks or months after the first, but is almost always less severe and shorter than the first episode.

Diagnosis

Doctors can **diagnose** genital herpes by a visual inspection if the outbreak is typical, and also by taking a sample from the sore or sores. However, it is difficult to diagnose between outbreaks, and blood tests do not always provide a definite answer. If an infected woman gives birth while the virus is active, the baby runs a slight risk of getting a deadly infection. Also, people infected with herpes both pass on and receive the **HIV** infection more easily, so they should be aware of this risk as soon as possible.

Treatment

There is no treatment that can cure herpes, but **antiviral** medications can shorten—or even prevent—an outbreak while the person takes the medicine.

Cold sores on the lips develop from a type of herpes infection. Genital herpes, however, is less obvious and harder to detect.

Gonorrhea

Gonorrhea is caused by *Neisseria gonorrhoea*, a **bacterium** that can grow and multiply easily in the **mucous membranes** of the body. Gonorrhea **bacteria** can grow in the warm, moist areas of the reproductive tract, including the cervix (opening to the womb), uterus (womb), and Fallopian tubes (egg canals) in women, and in the urethra (urine canal) in women and men. The bacteria can also grow in the mouth, throat, and anus.

Symptoms

The first **symptoms** of gonorrhea usually appear two to five days after **infection,** but it can take as long as 30 days for symptoms to begin.

Most infected men first notice a burning sensation while urinating and a yellowish white **discharge** from the penis. Men with gonorrhea sometimes have painful or swollen testicles. Women often do not notice similar early symptoms, or they mistake them for a bladder infection or yeast infection.

Diagnosis

A quick laboratory test for gonorrhea that can be done in the clinic or doctor's office is a Gram stain. A doctor or laboratory technician takes a small sample from the discharge. Staining the sample lets the doctor see the gonorrhea bacteria under a microscope. This test works better for men than for women. Another method is to take a sample and place it in a laboratory dish to see whether the bacteria grow and reproduce.

Treatment

Many of the currently used **antibiotics** can successfully cure gonorrhea. One of the most common antibiotics, penicillin, is no longer used to treat gonorrhea. That is because many strains of the gonorrhea bacterium have become **resistant** to penicillin. Although medication will stop the infection, it will not repair any permanent damage done by the disease.

It is important to treat gonorrhea as soon as possible; otherwise, it can lead to a range of serious complications. These include pelvic inflammatory disease, a sometimes fatal condition for women. Gonorrhea can spread to the blood or joints, putting the person's life in danger. Also, people with gonorrhea are more likely to contract the **HIV** infection. All of these risks can be passed on to the next generation because a pregnant woman may give the infection to her infant as the baby passes through the birth canal during delivery.

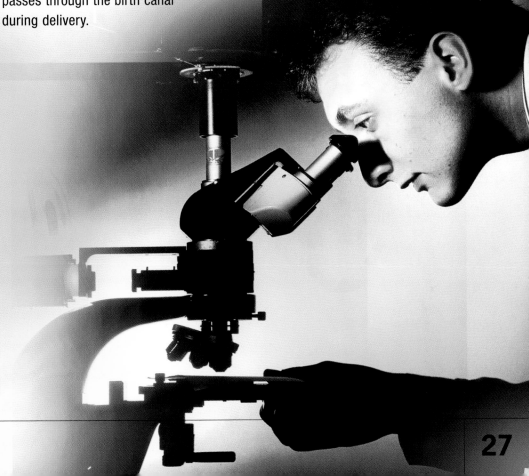

Medical personnel rely on microscopes to detect—and sometimes help treat—the wide range of STDs caused by organisms that are too small to be seen by the naked eye.

Hepatitis B

Hepatitis is an **inflammation** of the liver that can be caused by viruses, certain medications, and alcohol abuse. There are five viral forms of hepatitis (all known by letters); hepatitis B is the most dangerous. This is the form that is sexually transmitted and it is highly **contagious.** Many people have hepatitis B and pass it on to others without even knowing that they have the condition. Up to one in ten people with hepatitis B develops chronic hepatitis, which can lead to permanent liver damage and an increased risk of liver cancer.

Symptoms

Hepatitis B **symptoms** begin with fever, usually followed by weakness, loss of appetite, and muscle pains. The upper abdomen may be painful and tender. **Jaundice** appears gradually, reaching a peak at two weeks.

Diagnosis

Because of the complexity and the chemical differences of the virus, doctors perform a number of tests for hepatitis B. The three most common are all blood tests, which assess the presence of the **virus** in the blood and, if a virus is present, how fast it is replicating.

Treatment

Although hepatitis B has no cure, a vaccine against the disease is available. In the United States, the Centers for Disease Control and Prevention and other public health officials recommend **vaccination** for all infants and young adults. Young adults need to protect themselves before they become sexually active and possibly exposed to hepatitis B.

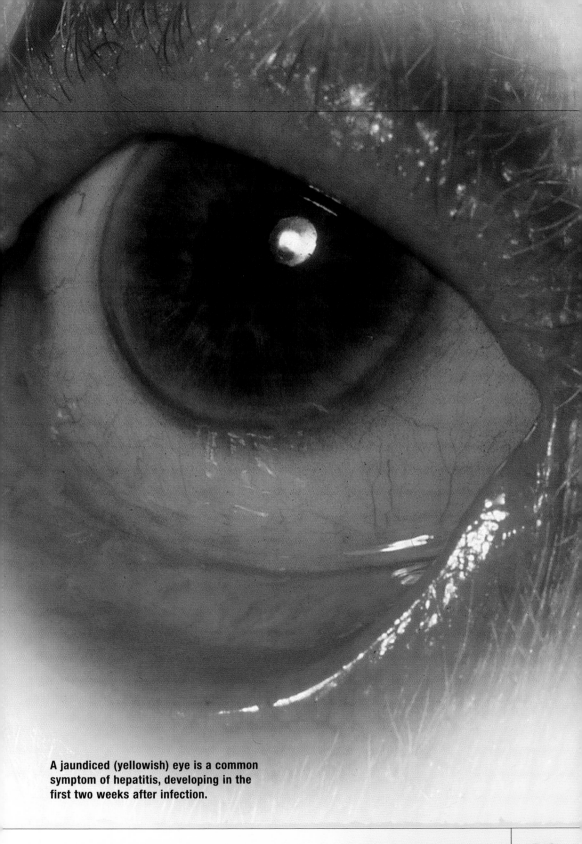

A jaundiced (yellowish) eye is a common symptom of hepatitis, developing in the first two weeks after infection.

Pubic lice

Pubic lice are tiny insects that can **infest** the pubic hair and survive by feeding on human blood. They are sometimes called crab lice or simply crabs. These **parasites** are usually spread by sexual contact, although they may also be picked up through contact with infested bedding or clothing.

Symptoms

The main **symptom** of infestation is itching in the pubic area. Scratching may spread the lice to other parts of the body. For this reason, anyone affected by pubic lice should avoid touching the infected area, although this may be difficult.

Diagnosis

Grayish, oval-shaped pubic lice are actually visible to the naked eye. They appear reddish-brown when full of blood from feeding. Nits, the tiny white eggs, are also visible. They tend to cling to the base of pubic hair.

Treatment

Lotions and shampoos to kill pubic lice are available both over the counter and by **prescription.** Most of them contain lindane, a powerful **pesticide.** Some doctors and pharmacists recommend using shampoos designed for treating head lice since the active ingredients are similar. People often prefer to ask for head lice treatment because it is less embarrassing. The itching sometimes continues even after the lice have been killed. This is because the skin has been irritated and requires time to heal.

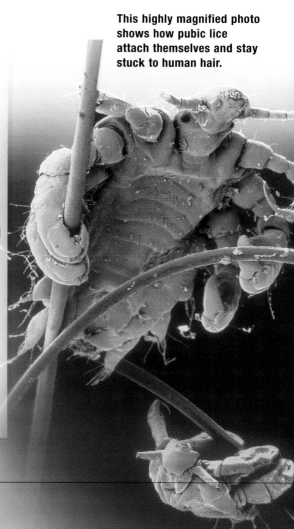

This highly magnified photo shows how pubic lice attach themselves and stay stuck to human hair.

Syphilis

Syphilis has often been called "the great imitator" because so many of the signs and symptoms are so like those of other diseases. It is caused by the **bacterium** *Treponema pallidum* and spreads from person to person through direct contact with a syphilis sore. If left untreated, it can pass through three stages—sometimes unnoticed—and can lead to death.

Symptoms

The first-stage symptom is a small sore (called a chancre sore) that appears at the spot where syphilis entered the body. It lasts up to six weeks, and it will heal on its own, although the infection is still there. The second stage features rashes on the hands and feet as well as fever, sore throat, hair loss, headaches, and tiredness. Third-stage signs and symptoms include not being able to coordinate muscle movements, paralysis, numbness, gradual blindness, and **dementia.** This damage may be serious enough to cause death.

Diagnosis

Shortly after **infection** occurs, the body produces syphilis **antibodies.** An accurate and inexpensive blood test can detect these antibodies and confirm the presence of syphilis.

Treatment

A single dose of penicillin, an **antibiotic,** will usually cure a person who has had syphilis for less than a year. Larger doses are needed to cure someone who has had it for longer than a year. Penicillin treatment will kill the syphilis bacterium and prevent further damage, but it will not repair any damage already done.

This patient shows symptoms of second-stage syphilis.

Life with STDs

Being **diagnosed** with a sexually transmitted disease almost always comes as something of a shock, even if it has been detected early on and can be treated easily. People sometimes view this news as a punishment. STDs, after all, can almost always be avoided by behaving sensibly and carefully (see pages 40–41). However, after the initial shock, the patient should be able to live a normal life within certain limits, especially once the **infection** is treated fully.

This swab is being placed in a culture dish to see whether STD-causing bacteria will be detected.

Firm action

After hearing the news, the first thing the patient should do is to seek out treatment as quickly as possible. This is particularly important for women because they run the risk of transmitting an STD to an infant either in childbirth or through breast milk. They should also tell all recent sexual partners and urge them to be tested for the STD. After receiving the medication, the patient should complete the course of treatment as **prescribed.** They should only use the medication prescribed for them, since the medicine and dosage might differ from person to person even when treating the same STD.

Treatment and beyond

During their course of treatment, the STD patient should take great care, remembering that the STD infection can pass to other parts of the body as well as to other people. For example, gonorrhea infection can spread to other unlikely parts of the body. A person can get an eye infection after touching infected genitals and then the eyes.

The patient should also avoid all sexual activity while being treated for the STD. Even after the course of treatment has ended and there are no obvious signs of the STD remaining, the patient should have a follow-up test to ensure that the infection has been cured. It is only then that the person can have sexual relations again, and this time they will have to be aware of the need for safe sex and other precautions.

Washing your hands will lessen the chance of STDs spreading from one part of your body to another.

Famous victim

Bacterial STDs, such as syphilis and gonorrhea, can now be treated fully and even cured. In some European countries, such as Sweden, they have been virtually eliminated. However, before these treatments became widespread, and at a time when STDs were not discussed or admitted openly, the diseases could take a deadly toll.

One of the most famous victims was Al Capone, the well-known Chicago gang leader. He ruled the Chicago network of organized crime in the 1920s with a combination of cunning and extreme violence. He was eventually convicted (of the lesser crime of tax evasion) in 1931 and spent eight years in prison.

By the time Capone was released, his past had come back to haunt him. Syphilis, which he had **contracted** years before, entered its advanced stages, and he spent his last eight years crippled and in great pain.

A lapse to regret

Alan (not his real name) is a college student in New York. His story shows how "letting your guard down" just once can have lasting consequences.

Alan has had a long-term relationship with another student, but over the winter break he met up with an ex-girlfriend in his home town.

"We had a little too much to drink and one thing led to another … and, well, we slept together 'for old times sake.' The next day we both felt a bit embarrassed about it all and I guess we both blamed it on the alcohol. I got back to New York about a week later and found an e-mail from my ex-girlfriend. She had been to a health clinic and had tested positive for gonorrhea. I nearly fell through the floor. I mean, my current girlfriend and I always practice safe sex, but that time back home just that once I hadn't.

"I've been avoiding telling my girlfriend and finding excuses not to see her, but I know I'll have to. Maybe I'll wait until I go and get checked out. If I've got it, I'll tell her. I don't want to infect her, but I don't want to split up. I guess this shows what that stuff about trust is all about."

The famous Chicago gangster Al Capone was brought down, not by a police officer's bullet, but by advanced syphilis.

Family and Friends

The subject of sex is often a difficult one for families to discuss. Many parents find it hard to imagine that their children have grown up enough to be considering a sexual relationship. Even if they have discussed sex in general, families often avoid talking about sexually transmitted diseases. This unwillingness to be open is very dangerous. Also, it makes it much harder for young people to admit having an STD if they have become infected.

Teenagers must sometimes take the lead in such discussions. If they feel they are old enough to consider having sex, then they should accept that there are many responsibilities that go along with it. One of these is to take the lead in discussions about sex if other family members will not.

Peer pressure

Health care workers dealing with STDs all agree that it is best to wait before you start to have sex. Having sex early in life usually means that you will end up having more sexual partners overall, and with more partners you increase your chances of developing a sexually transmitted disease. Many young people, however, find it hard to make this choice. Instead of listening to the medical advice, they are swayed by the pressure to have sex. This pressure comes from many sources: from movies and TV shows, from the words of pop songs, from commercials and advertisements, but most of all from their friends.

The teenage years are difficult for most people. Teenagers are almost adults and have many of the responsibilities that go with that. It is a time when most people are developing a separate identity, although they might still be a little uncertain about just what form that identity will take. Being insecure and inexperienced with this freedom, many people follow the examples of their friends. They don't want to feel left out or not cool, so they often decide to do things that they would not normally consider. This feeling of being forced to do something is called peer pressure. The word *peer* means those around you who are in the same position.

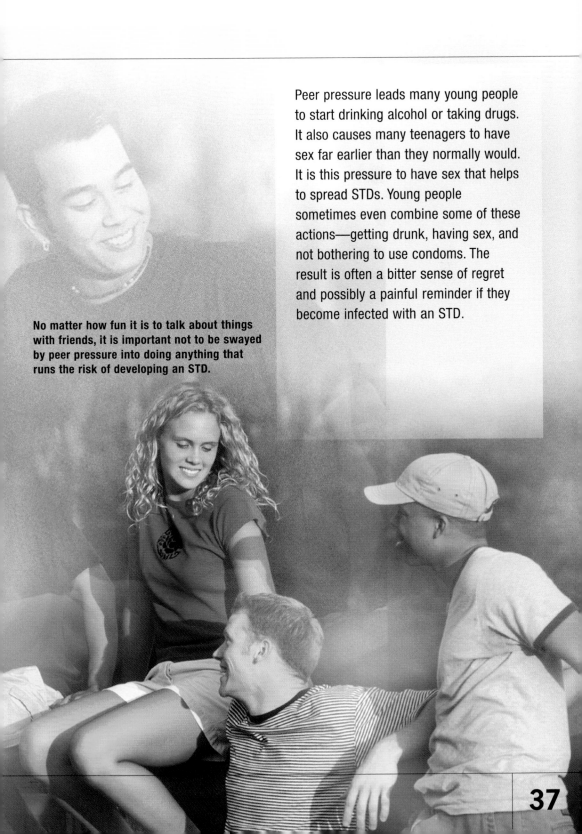

Peer pressure leads many young people to start drinking alcohol or taking drugs. It also causes many teenagers to have sex far earlier than they normally would. It is this pressure to have sex that helps to spread STDs. Young people sometimes even combine some of these actions—getting drunk, having sex, and not bothering to use condoms. The result is often a bitter sense of regret and possibly a painful reminder if they become infected with an STD.

No matter how fun it is to talk about things with friends, it is important not to be swayed by peer pressure into doing anything that runs the risk of developing an STD.

Dealing with pressure

The iwannaknow.org Web site, which deals with teen sex issues, offers the following advice for young people who need help dealing with peer pressure:

- go out with a group of friends rather than only your date
- think of what you would say in advance in case someone tries to pressure you
- be ready to call your mom, dad, or a friend to pick you up if you need to leave a date
- never feel obligated to "pay someone back" with sex in return for an expensive date or gift
- say "no" and mean "no" if that's how you feel

The "special relationship"

The friend whose opinion should matter most, of course, is your girlfriend or boyfriend. If you are mature enough to have a sexual relationship, one of the most important things to do is communicate. A person should feel free to discuss concerns about getting an STD. One partner could start the conversation by stating that he or she cares about the health and well-being of both persons. People deciding to have sex with a new partner should discuss ways of protecting each other. Again, honesty is the best policy.

Most STDs are readily treated, so the earlier a person warns sexual partners about the disease, the less likely the disease is to be spread. If the person does have an STD, then an honest admission lets the partner seek early—and usually effective—treatment. Otherwise, the STD could do irreparable physical damage, be spread to others or, in the case of a woman, be passed on to a newborn baby.

The strongest relationships are built and maintained through a sense of mutual trust.

Control and Prevention

The twin issues of control and prevention lead the fight against sexually transmitted diseases. Together they can help reduce the spread of STDs, increase success rates among the curable diseases, and limit the occurrence of incurable STDs such as herpes. The responsibility for control falls mainly on national governments, international health organizations, and the many charities and public-awareness groups that focus on STDs. Prevention, however, is an area where individuals should play the leading role.

Wider efforts

As in so many areas, the issue of STD prevention is tied in with the efforts to combat **HIV** and **AIDS infection.** The lessons from AIDS (see pages 42–45) should help these prevention efforts. The most important of these is the call for safe sex—using condoms or avoiding intercourse outright in favor of cuddling and other demonstrations of affection. These same actions can significantly reduce the spread of STDs generally.

Medical personnel and **public health** officials believe that education is the key to controlling the spread of STDs. No matter how many new treatments—or possible cures—are developed, the public needs to be made aware of this progress. In this way, dozens of government and private organizations are making STD information freely available (see pages 52–53). Newspaper and magazine articles, in addition to television coverage, help to get this message across.

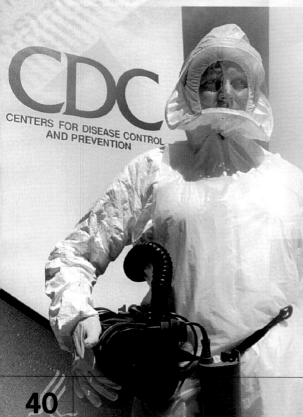

CDC
CENTERS FOR DISEASE CONTROL AND PREVENTION

The Centers for Disease Control and Prevention (CDC), in Atlanta, is the headquarters for many U.S.-based prevention efforts.

Personal responsibility

Knowing about STDs and their effects is one thing, but the real key for individuals is avoiding infection in the first place. The actions of individual people are the most important factors in halting the spread of these diseases. It is vital to learn the common **symptoms** of STDs and to seek medical help immediately if any symptoms develop, even if they are mild.

The best way to prevent STDs, of course, is to avoid sexual contact with others. Delay having sexual relations as long as possible. The younger people are when they have sex for the first time, the more likely they are to develop an STD. The risk of acquiring an STD also increases with the number of sexual partners over a lifetime. Those who do decide to be sexually active should stay with one partner who they know is not infected. Whenever they do have sex, they should use a male condom. They should also have regular check-ups for STDs—especially if having sex with a new partner—even if there are no obvious symptoms.

Every young person, both male and female, should become familiar with how to use condoms, which are vital in preventing the spread of STDs.

Lessons from HIV and AIDS

By far the most widely known—and deadliest—of all sexually transmitted diseases is **HIV,** which leads to **AIDS.** In the two decades since it was first identified on a global scale, this disease has mobilized support from international organizations and led many governments to re-think their policies on the whole issue of **public health.** Most of the statistics surrounding AIDS are frightening. Perhaps the most alarming is the number of people carrying the **infection** that leads to AIDS—40 million worldwide at the beginning of 2002.

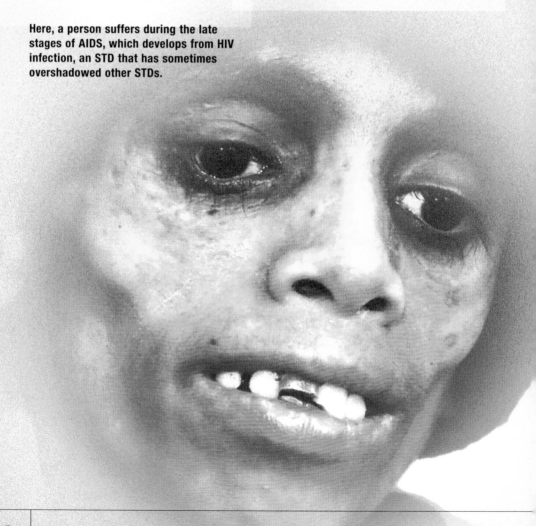

Here, a person suffers during the late stages of AIDS, which develops from HIV infection, an STD that has sometimes overshadowed other STDs.

The scope of the AIDS disease—and the worldwide battle against it—should have alerted people to the dangers of all STDs. The question is: Are people any wiser about STDs in general, or has AIDS distracted their attention? The answer seems to fall somewhere in between. People now know much more about AIDS than they did in the 1980s. Yet has this knowledge led to more awareness of other STDs? It appears not—many people still remain uninformed about the transmission and treatment of even the most common STDs. Despite efforts to raise public awareness about how STDs are spread, much more still needs to be done.

Fading from view

In the late 1970s and early 1980s, people placing newspaper ads for partners would add "herpes positive" or "herpes negative" to indicate whether they carried the herpes **virus** described on page 25. At that time, herpes—incurable and spreading fast—seemed to strike terror among most young people. Yet within a few years, when the first AIDS casualties became known, people began wondering "Whatever happened to herpes?" The truth, of course, is that nothing had happened to the viral infection. More people were becoming infected, but the problem seemed to fade from view in the face of such deadly competition. The lingering discomfort of herpes did not earn the same headline space as certain death, which is how AIDS was portrayed.

People had not chosen to ignore what had once seemed to be such a huge problem, it just became overshadowed. The same can be said for many other STDs, including syphilis, gonorrhea, and chlamydial infection. According to a 2001 public health survey of sexually active U.S. teens, half said they know someone with an STD. Yet among teens who have had sexual intercourse, only 50 percent realize the risk of contracting an STD. Could part of the problem be that, distracted by the terrible fear of HIV and AIDS, people have lost interest in keeping informed about other STDs—how they spread and how they are treated?

Getting the message

Doctors and other health officials cannot be blamed if people have "let their guard down" about STDs other than **HIV** and **AIDS**. In fact, most medical information insists on grouping HIV and AIDS with other STDs, so that people can view these diseases for what they are: dangerous infections passed on largely through sexual relations.

The **public health** campaigns to slow the spread of AIDS all over the world have also stressed that AIDS prevention helps control other STDs. One of the central messages in this body of advice is safe sex—avoiding unprotected sexual contact and always using a condom. This, of course, reinforces the advice for preventing STDs of all kind, so the AIDS message has worked in that respect. Also, people at risk are urged to have regular tests for HIV **infection.**

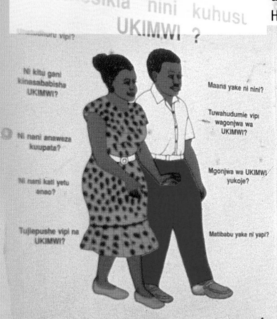

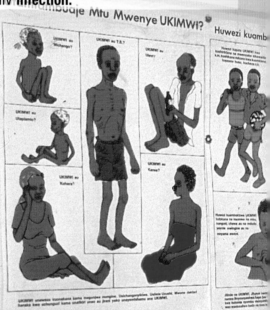

Double-edged sword?

Increased awareness about HIV and AIDS and other STDs is a good thing, and so is the ability to be checked regularly for HIV infection. After all, someone going in for an HIV test will usually be willing to be tested for other STDs. However, a number of problems occur with this process. What if an HIV test proves positive, indicating that the person does carry the HIV infection? Many people view such knowledge as a death sentence, and perhaps the fear of such news would stop them from even trying to find out. Without being checked for HIV, they could also be letting other STD infections develop. That would be bad enough, but carrying certain STD infections—especially chlamydial infection—actually makes someone more likely to become infected with HIV.

This AIDS education poster, on display in a Tanzanian hospital, provides clear and vivid descriptions of how the HIV infection can spread as well as examples of common symptoms.

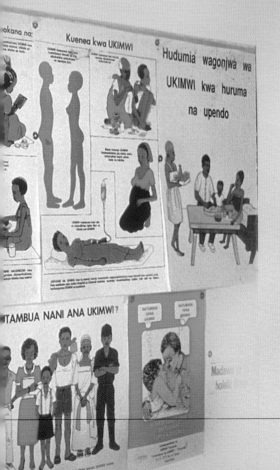

Treatment and Counseling

Awareness lies at the root of the battle against sexually transmitted diseases. Because preventing the diseases is all about behavior and attitude—being open with partners, having safe sex, and using protection—treatment is often aimed at the same organ, the brain. Very often the treatment, and the counseling sessions linked with it, is the first chance for patients to understand STDs clearly.

When in doubt

People who think they might have an STD should not try to **diagnose** or treat themselves. Only a doctor or other trained health professional can do those things. There is a wide range of STD treatment available in most countries. Anyone who thinks they have an STD can contact a local clinic, private doctor, family-planning clinic, or hospital. It is important to remember that services are totally **confidential.** No one will know that a person has been to a clinic or a doctor unless that person tells others.

First of all, the person should tell the doctor or health care professional why they think they might have an STD. There are special tests that can tell whether someone has an STD. Often, it is enough to test a small sample of blood taken from the patient's arm. Sometimes, fluid is taken from the genitals or other exposed areas with a cotton swab.

Sometimes a doctor can tell right away if a person has an STD. Otherwise, the doctor must wait several days for the full test results. Treatment, however, may begin on the first visit. Except for **AIDS,** genital herpes, and viral hepatitis, most other STDs can be cured easily and quickly. Not all STDs are treated in the same way. The doctor might use **prescription** drugs, injections, or creams. Remember, though, that the choice of treatment depends on the person as well as the disease. That means that it is crucial that no one should ever take someone else's prescribed medicine. Doing so could lead to serious side effects and the **infection** could be covered up but not cured.

Getting the facts right

One of the benefits of front-line treatment and counseling is that health care professionals can use these sessions to increase awareness about STDs. It is not surprising that anyone who goes to the doctor or health care professional about an STD will be interested to learn about how they are passed on and treated. What is shocking, though, is the level of ignorance many of these same people display when they first walk through the door.

The Centers for Disease Control and Prevention (CDC) is one of the leading authorities about STDs and other **infectious** diseases. It recently completed a study of 3,500 STD clinic visitors to check on people's knowledge and attitudes about STDs.

After examining a patient, a doctor will usually discuss his or her case history before writing out a prescription for STD treatment.

The results were alarming. Many individuals—even patients receiving treatment—had misguided notions of how to protect themselves from STDs. When they were first interviewed, nearly half of the study participants believed **douching** protected against STDs, approximately 40 percent thought urinating after sex prevented STDs, 20 percent believed birth control pills protected against STDs, and 16 percent thought washing their genitals after sex was effective protection.

It was only after several counseling sessions that these misinformed patients began to show a clearer understanding about STDs. About half of those who originally had misconceptions were no longer misguided when they completed a survey three months after their clinic visit.

The value of openness

The CDC study offers some hope that, with proper counseling, even the most misinformed people can reach a better understanding of STDs. However, better understanding is not enough to prevent STDs. It is essential that people are open with their sexual partners about their own medical history. People with an STD should be sure that their partners receive medical care so they do not become seriously ill. Also, treatment of the partner will keep the person from getting reinfected if sex with that partner resumes.

Young people should be encouraged to visit health clinics regularly, with or without a parent or guardian.

Children and parents

The Queensland Law Reform Commission in Australia has addressed a problem that has troubled people all over the world: Should young people be able to seek STD treatment without their parents' permission? Like all 50 U.S. states and many other governments, it concludes that the answer is "yes."

"It is necessary to choose between two evils: (a) inadequate treatment and (b) concealing information from parents that is relevant to the care and upbringing of their child. In our opinion, (b) is the lesser evil. Thus, we believe children should be able to consent to **diagnosis** and treatment of sexually transmissible diseases."

"Counselors can help patients replace their misconceptions with more effective strategies for STD protection."

(Richard A. Crosby, of the Division of STD Prevention at the Centers for Disease Control and Prevention)

Doctors take a professional vow to guard the privacy of their dealings with patients.

People to Talk To

The best people to talk to about STDs and other sexual matters are your parents. It is easy to forget that your parents' experiences could help them to help you. Unfortunately, parents often find the subject as embarrassing to discuss as their children do. Instead, many young people find out about sex from their friends, and this information is often inaccurate or even totally wrong (see pages 36–39).

The United States has one of the highest rates of STD **infection** in the world—far higher than in many European countries where the subject of sex is discussed more openly. A survey in the United States found that mothers of children aged eleven and older rated themselves "unsatisfactory" when discussing issues such as: how to tell when you are ready to be sexually active (38 percent), preventing **HIV** (40 percent), **sexual orientation** (47 percent), and how to use a condom (73 percent).

Other sources

If communication at home is difficult, where can you turn? The best people are those who have had experience with discussing sexual matters. Teachers and youth group organizers are usually well informed about STDs. Their years of experience dealing with young people also makes them value the need for honesty and **confidentiality** in this area. A number of other adults—including doctors, nurses, and counselors—are often willing to talk to young people about this important subject.

One of the best ways of preventing the spread of STDs is discussing them openly with young people, without letting peer pressure cloud the issue.

Wherever you live, you can find a wide range of telephone contacts—many of them toll-free and most of them **anonymous**—where you can find out more about STDs and other sexual matters. Many of the organizations listed in the "Information and Advice" section (pages 52–53) provide advice over the telephone, and they can suggest local clinics or health centers in your immediate area. Others are geared specifically to questions coming from younger people. Whether you approach one of these organizations, or a family member, a youth leader, or teacher, the important thing is to be able to talk—and listen—freely about your concerns. Sharing a problem or worry is the first step to solving it.

❝The American Social Health Association strongly believes that 'sexuality education begins at home' and that a parent is a child's 'most important sexuality educator.'❞

(From the ASHA website)

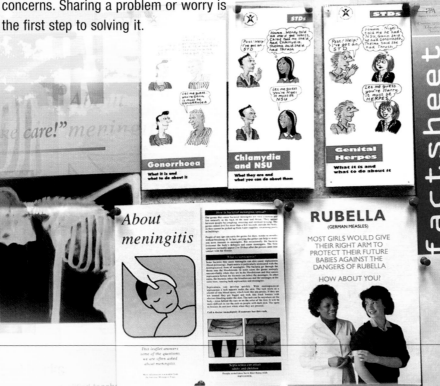

Information and Advice

The following organizations have a special interest in providing information and advice about STDs. Several deal primarily with the issues of HIV infection and AIDS, but even these provide useful information about STDs in general. The listings below can provide exact advice for specific locations within the country. Many of these organizations operate almost exclusively over the Internet, so Web site addresses are listed in addition to (where relevant) telephone numbers and addresses.

Advocates for Youth
1025 Vermont Avenue NW
Washington, DC 20005
(202) 347-5700
Advocates for Youth tackles problems relating to a wide range of young people's concerns, and its information on STDs is up-to-date and informative.

The American Social
Health Association (ASHA)
(800) 227-8922
This voluntary organization, dedicated to the prevention and control of all STDs, operates the National Sexually Transmitted Disease Hotline. Trained counselors answer questions about all STDs.

The Centers for Disease Control and
Prevention (CDC)
www.cdc.gov
Located in Atlanta, Georgia, CDC is an agency of the Department of Health and Human Services. Its aim is to promote health and quality of life by preventing and controlling disease, injury, and disability.

CDC National Prevention
Information Network
www.cdcnpin.org
The CDC oversees this service for the National Center for HIV, STD, and TB Prevention. The site contains easily accessible information, particularly about completed campaigns against STDs.

iwannaknow
www.iwannaknow.org
This Web site, operated in conjunction with ASHA, is designed specifically for teenagers. It has detailed information about all the major STDs as well as links to many other sites and a lively forum.

unspeakable
www.unspeakable.com
This confidential site enables users to identify their own risk for STDs, test their knowledge about different kinds of STDs, and receive information on the latest treatments. There is a database of nearly 4,000 STD clinics around the country and a section on frequently asked questions (FAQs).

More Books To Read

Byers, Ann. *Sexually Transmitted Diseases*. Berkeley Heights, NJ: Enslow Publishers, 1999.

Curran, Christine Perdan. *Sexually Transmitted Diseases*. Berkeley Heights, NJ: Enslow Publishers, 1998.

Endersbe, Julie. *Sexually Transmitted Diseases: How Are They Prevented?*. Mankato, Minn.: Capstone Press, 2000.

Endersbe, Julie. *Teen Sex: Risks and Consequences*. Mankato, Minn.: Capstone Press, 2000.

Little, Marjorie. *Sexually Transmitted Diseases*. Broomall, Penn.: Chelsea House, 1991.

Nardo, Don. *Teen Sexuality*. San Diego, Ca.: Lucent Books,1997.

Peacock, Judith. *Birth Control and Protection: Options for Teens*. Mankato, Minn.: Capstone Press, 2000.

Storad, Conrad. *Inside AIDS*. Minneapolis, Minn.: Lerner Publishing Group, 1998.

White, Katherine. *Everything You Need to Know about AIDS and HIV*. New York: Rosen Publishing Group, 2001.

Glossary

acupuncture
type of Chinese medical treatment that uses needles inserted in certain parts of the body

AIDS
(Acquired Immunodeficiency Syndrome)
deadly condition that prevents the body from defending itself against disease, gained from infection by HIV

anonymous
unknown

antibiotic
medical chemical that stops the growth of, or kills, bacteria

antibodies
naturally produced chemicals that fight off infection

antiviral
designed to treat attacks by viruses

archaeologist
person who studies human history

bacteria
plural of bacterium

bacterium
tiny one-celled organism

compound
chemical substance made up of two or more elements

confidential
with a respect for one's privacy

confidentiality
state of being confidential

contagious
(of a disease) able to be spread by bodily contact

contract
to acquire something (such as a disease)

dementia
severe loss of intelligence because of harm to the brain

diagnose
to determine whether a medical condition exists

diagnosis
identification of a disease

discharge
something that has flowed out of an opening in the body

douching
washing and rinsing the sexual organs with a concentrated spray of water

epidemic
contagious disease that spreads rapidly

epididimytis
unnatural swelling of a man's sexual organs

fungal
relating to fungi

fungi
tiny organisms that resemble plants but cannot produce their own food

heterosexual
being attracted to people of the opposite sex

HIV
(Human Immunodeficiency Virus)
virus that causes AIDS

infection
act of being affected by a disease

infectious
causing infection

infertility
inability to have children

infest
to live in or on something as a parasite

inflammation
painful and tender swelling

irreparable
damaged beyond repair

jaundice
yellowing of the skin caused by the build-up of bile in the blood

medieval
referring to the Middle Ages

monitor
to watch over constantly and often under medical supervision

mucous membrane
cells in the body that produce mucus

mucus
slimy substance produced by the body to protect it against attack

organism
living animal, plant, or single-celled life form

parasite
organism that feeds off another organism

pesticide
chemical used to destroy plant, animal, or fungal pests

plague
infectious disease, caused by a bacterium, that killed millions of people in the 14th century

prescription
request for medicine made by a doctor

public health
dealing with the control and prevention of diseases in a city or country

reportable
(of a disease) needing to be reported to medical authorities if it is diagnosed

reproductive system
human organs that produce sperm (male) and eggs (female)

resistant
able to withstand treatment that once destroyed it

sexual orientation
whether someone is attracted to people of the same sex (homosexuality) or the opposite sex (heterosexuality)

symptom
outward signs of a disease or condition

urinary tract
organs of the body that rid the system of liquid waste (urine)

vaccination
injection that prevents people from being infected by a certain virus

venereal diseases
former name for sexually transmitted diseases

virus
tiny object that causes infection by making copies of itself inside another organism

Index

A antibiotics 13, 22, 24, 26, 31
antibodies 31
antiviral medications 25

B babies, infecting 8, 20, 21, 24, 25, 27,
32, 38
bacterial STDs 4, 7, 13, 22–23, 24,
26, 31, 34
blisters and sores 25, 31

C cancers 8, 21, 28
Capone, Al 34, 35
chlamydial infection 10, 11, 23, 24, 43, 45
clinics 46, 48
condoms 12, 15, 19, 37, 40, 41, 44, 50
confidentiality 4, 46, 50
control and prevention 4, 8, 19, 40–41,
44, 48
counseling 46, 47, 48
crabs, see pubic lice

D death 31
discharge 24, 26

E epidemics 10, 20
epididymitis 24

F family and friends 36–38, 49, 50
fungal and yeast infections 7, 23

G genital herpes 23, 25, 46
gonorrhea 4, 6, 10, 11, 12, 13, 20, 23, 24,
26–27, 33, 34, 43

H hepatitis B 11, 23, 28, 29, 46
herpes virus 16, 25, 43
HIV/AIDS 4, 8, 11, 16–17, 19, 25, 27, 40,
42, 43, 44, 45, 46
human papilloma virus (HPV) 21

I infertility 8, 21
information and advice 50–53

P peer pressure 36–37, 38
pelvic inflammatory disease (PID) 8, 10, 21,
24, 27
penicillin 13, 26, 31
protective devices 12, 15, 19, 41, 44, 46

pubic lice 7, 23, 30
public awareness 16, 18, 20, 42, 43,
45, 47
public health campaigns 16, 40, 42, 44

S safe sex 19, 33, 34, 40, 44, 46
sex, pressure to have 36–37, 38
sexual partners
number of 6, 7, 36, 41
telling 32, 38, 48
sexually transmitted diseases (STDs)
causes 7, 22–23
contracting 4, 6, 7, 12, 13, 16, 19,
20–21, 22–23
economic costs 11
highest-risk group 19
history of 12–15
ignorance about 4, 6, 18, 47, 48
risks for women 8, 20, 21, 32
side effects 8, 10, 21
statistics 10, 11, 19, 42
testing for 7, 19, 24, 32, 41, 44, 45, 46
viral STDs 4, 7, 13, 16, 23, 25,
28, 43
symptoms 7, 8, 22, 41
syphilis 4, 6, 10, 11, 12, 13, 15, 20, 23, 31,
34, 43

T talking about the issue 50–51
telephone helplines 51
treatment 8, 32–33, 46–47
children and parental permission 49
trichomoniasis 10

U urination, painful 26

V vaccinations 23, 28
venereal diseases see sexually transmitted
diseases (STDs)

W women 8, 20, 21, 32
infertility 8, 21
reproductive system 8, 21